# LUSTRA

OF

## EZRA POUND

*Definition*—" LUSTRUM : an offering for the sins of the whole people, made by the censors at the expiration of their five years of office."
*Elementary Latin Dictionary of Charlton T. Lewis.*

200 *copies privately printed, of which this is No.* . .

CERTAIN of these poems have appeared in *Poetry*, *Blast, Poetry and Drama, Smart Set,* and *Others,* to the editors of which magazines the author wishes to make due acknowledgment.

E. P.

## V. L.

*Cui dono lepidum novum libellum.*

# CONTENTS

| | PAGE | | PAGE |
|---|---|---|---|
| Tenzone | 9 | The Bath Tub | 38 |
| The Condolence | 10 | Amitiés | 39 |
| The Garret | 11 | Meditatio | 41 |
| The Garden | 12 | To Dives | 41 |
| Ortus | 13 | Ladies | 42 |
| Salutation | 14 | Phyllidula | 44 |
| Salutation the Second | 15 | The Patterns | 44 |
| The Spring | 17 | Coda | 44 |
| Albâtre | 18 | The Seeing Eye | 45 |
| Causa | 18 | Ancora | 46 |
| Commission | 19 | " Dompna pois de me no'us | |
| A Pact | 21 | cal " | 47 |
| Surgit Fama | 22 | The Coming of War: | |
| Preference | 23 | Actaeon | 50 |
| Dance Figure | 24 | After Ch'u Yuan | 51 |
| April | 26 | Liu Ch'e | 51 |
| Gentildonna | 26 | Fan-piece, for her Imperial | |
| The Rest | 27 | Lord | 52 |
| Les Millwin | 28 | Ts'ai Chi'h | 52 |
| Further Instructions | 29 | In a Station of the Metro | 53 |
| A Song of the Degrees | 30 | Alba | 53 |
| Ite | 31 | Heather | 53 |
| Dum Capitolium Scandet | 31 | The Faun | 54 |
| To Καλόν | 31 | Coitus | 54 |
| The Study in Aesthetics | 32 | The Encounter | 55 |
| The Bellaires | 33 | Tempora | 55 |
| The New Cake of Soap | 35 | Black Slippers: Bellotti | 56 |
| Salvationists | 36 | Society | 56 |
| Epitaph | 37 | Image from D'Orleans | 57 |
| Arides | 37 | Papyrus | 57 |

# CONTENTS

| | PAGE |
|---|---|
| "Ione, Dead the Long Year" | 57 |
| ἱμέρρω. . . . . . | 58 |
| Shop Girl . . . . . | 58 |
| To Formianus' Young Lady Friend . . . . . . | 59 |
| Tame Cat. . . . . . | 60 |
| L'Art, 1910 . . . . . | 60 |
| Simulacra . . . . . | 61 |
| Women before a Shop . . | 61 |
| Epilogue . . . . . . | 62 |
| The Social Order . . . | 63 |
| The Tea Shop . . . . | 64 |
| Epitaphs . . . . . . | 65 |
| Our Contemporaries . . | 65 |
| Ancient Wisdom, Rather Cosmic. . . . . . | 66 |
| The Three Poets . . . | 66 |
| The Gipsy . . . . . | 67 |
| The Game of Chess. . . | 68 |
| Provincia Deserta . . . | 69 |

**CATHAY**

| | |
|---|---|
| Song of the Bowmen of Shu . . . . . . | 75 |
| The Beautiful Toilet. . | 77 |
| The River Song . . . | 78 |
| The River Merchant's Wife: A Letter . . | 81 |
| The Jewel Stairs' Grievance . . . . | 83 |
| Poem by the Bridge at Ten-Shin . . . . | 84 |

| | PAGE |
|---|---|
| Lament of the Frontier Guard . . . . . | 86 |
| Exile's Letter. . . . | 88 |
| Four Poems of Departure Separation on the River Kiang. . . . . | 93 |
| Taking Leave of a Friend . . . . | 93 |
| Leave-taking near Shoku. . . . . | 94 |
| The City of Choan. . | 95 |
| South Folk in Cold Country . . . . . | 96 |
| Sennin Poem by Kakuhaku | 97 |
| A Ballad of the Mulberry Road . . . . . . | 98 |
| Old Idea of Choan by Rosoriu . . . . | 99 |
| To-Em-Mei's "The Unmoving Cloud" . . . | 101 |
| Near Perigord . . . . | 103 |
| Villanelle: The Psychological Hour . . . . . | 112 |
| Dans un Omnibus de Londres . . . . . | 115 |
| To a Friend Writing on Cabaret Dancers . . . | 117 |
| Homage to Quintus Septimius Florentis Christianus . . . . . . | 121 |
| Fish and the Shadow . . | 123 |

# LUSTRA OF EZRA POUND

## Tenzone

WILL people accept them ?
       (i.e. these songs).
As a timorous wench from a centaur
      (or a centurion),
Already they flee, howling in terror.

Will they be touched with the verisimilitudes ?
      Their virgin stupidity is untemptable.
I beg you, my friendly critics,
Do not set about to procure me an audience.

I mate with my free kind upon the crags ;
      the hidden recesses
Have heard the echo of my heels,
      in the cool light,
      in the darkness.

# The Condolence

*A mis soledades voy,*
*De mis soledades vengo,*
*Porque por andar conmigo*
*Mi bastan mis pensamientos.*
                    Lope de Vega.

O MY fellow sufferers, songs of my youth,
A lot of asses praise you because you are " virile,"
We, you, I !   We are " Red Bloods " !
Imagine it, my fellow sufferers—
Our maleness lifts us out of the ruck,
        Who'd have foreseen it ?

O my fellow sufferers, we went out under the
    trees,
We were in especial bored with male stupidity.
We went forth gathering delicate thoughts,
Our "*fantastikon*" delighted to serve us.
We were not exasperated with women,
        for the female is ductile.

And now you hear what is said to us :
We are compared to that sort of person
Who wanders about announcing his sex
As if he had just discovered it.
Let us leave this matter, my songs,
        and return to that which concerns us.

# The Garret

COME let us pity those who are better off than
   we are.
Come, my friend, and remember
      that the rich have butlers and no friends,
And we have friends and no butlers.
Come let us pity the married and the unmarried.

Dawn enters with little feet
      like a gilded Pavlova,
And I am near my desire.
Nor has life in it aught better
Than this hour of clear coolness,
      the hour of waking together.

# The Garden

*En robe de parade.*
Samain.

LIKE a skein of loose silk blown against a wall
She walks by the railing of a path in Kensington
Gardens,
And she is dying piece-meal
of a sort of emotional anæmia.

And round about there is a rabble
Of the filthy, sturdy, unkillable infants of the
very poor.
They shall inherit the earth.

In her is the end of breeding.
Her boredom is exquisite and excessive.
She would like someone to speak to her,
And is almost afraid that I
will commit that indiscretion.

# Ortus

How have I laboured ?
How have I not laboured
To bring her soul to birth,
To give these elements a name and a centre !

She is beautiful as the sunlight, and as fluid.
She has no name, and no place.
How have I laboured to bring her soul into
  separation ;
To give her a name and her being !

Surely you are bound and entwined,
You are mingled with the elements unborn ;
I have loved a stream and a shadow.

I beseech you enter your life.
I beseech you learn to say " I "
When I question you :
For you are no part, but a whole ;
No portion, but a being.

# Salutation

O GENERATION of the thoroughly smug
                and thoroughly uncomfortable,
I have seen fishermen picnicking in the sun,
I have seen them with untidy families,
I have seen their smiles full of teeth
                and heard ungainly laughter.

And I am happier than you are,
And they were happier than I am;
And the fish swim in the lake
                and do not even own clothing.

## Salutation the Second

YOU were praised, my books,
      because I had just come from the country;

I was twenty years behind the times
      so you found an audience ready.

I do not disown you,
      do not you disown your progeny.

Here they stand without quaint devices,
Here they are with nothing archaic about them.

Watch the reporters spit,
Watch the anger of the professors,
Watch how the pretty ladies revile them:

" Is this," they say, " the nonsense
      that we expect of poets ? "

" Where is the Picturesque ? "
      " Where is the vertigo of emotion ? "

" No ! his first work was the best."
      " Poor Dear ! he has lost his illusions."

# SALUTATION THE SECOND

Go, little naked and impudent songs,
Go with a light foot!
(Or with two light feet, if it please you!)
Go and dance shamelessly!
Go with an impertinent frolic!

Greet the grave and the stodgy,
Salute them with your thumbs at your noses.

Here are your bells and confetti.
Go! rejuvenate things!
Rejuvenate even " The Spectator."
    Go! and make cat calls!
Dance and make people blush,
Dance the dance of the phallus
    and tell anecdotes of Cybele!
Speak of the indecorous conduct of the Gods!
    (Tell it to Mr. Strachey.)

Ruffle the skirts of prudes,
    speak of their knees and ankles.
But, above all, go to practical people—
    go! jangle their door-bells!
Say that you do no work
    and that you will live forever.

# The Spring

CYDONIAN spring with her attendant train,
Maelids and water-girls,
Stepping beneath a boisterous wind from Thrace,
Throughout this sylvan place
Spreads the bright tips,
And every vine-stock is
Clad in new brilliancies.
                              And wild desire
Falls like black lightning.
O bewildered heart;
Though every branch have back what last year
    lost,
She, who moved here amid the cyclamen,
Moves only now a clinging tenuous ghost.

# Albâtre

THIS lady in the white bath-robe which she calls
  a peignoir
Is, for the time being, the mistress of my friend,
And the delicate white feet of her little white
  dog
Are not more delicate than she is,
Nor would Gautier himself' have despised their
  contrasts in whiteness
As she sits in the great chair
Between the two indolent candles.

# Causa

I JOIN these words for four people,
Some others may overhear them,
O world, I am sorry for you,
You do not know these four people.

# Commission

Go, my songs, to the lonely and the unsatisfied,
Go also to the nerve-wracked, go to the enslaved-
  by-convention,
Bear to them my contempt for their oppressors.
Go as a great wave of cool water,
Bear my contempt of oppressors.

Speak against unconscious oppression,
Speak against the tyranny of the unimaginative,
Speak against bonds.

Go to the bourgeoise who is dying of her ennuis,
Go to the women in suburbs.

Go to the hideously wedded,
Go to them whose failure is concealed,
Go to the unluckily mated,
Go to the bought wife,
Go to the woman entailed.

Go to those who have delicate lust,
Go to those whose delicate desires are thwarted.

# COMMISSION

Go like a blight upon the dulness of the world ;
Go with your edge against this,
Strengthen the subtle cords,
Bring confidence upon the algae and the tentacles
 of the soul.

Go in a friendly manner,
Go with an open speech.
Be eager to find new evils and new good,
Be against all forms of oppression.
Go to those who are thickened with middle age,
To those who have lost their interest.

Go to the adolescent who are smothered in
 family—
Oh how hideous it is
To see three generations of one house gathered
 ` together !
It is like an old tree with shoots,
And with some branches rotted and falling.

Go out and defy opinion,
Go against this vegetable bondage of the blood.
Be against all sorts of mortmain.

# A Pact

I MAKE a pact with you, Walt Whitman—
I have detested you long enough.
I come to you as a grown child
Who has had a pig-headed father;
I am old enough now to make friends.
It was you that broke the new wood,
Now is a time for carving.
We have one sap and one root—
Let there be commerce between us.

# Surgit Fama

THERE is a truce among the gods,
Korè is seen in the North
Skirting the blue-gray sea
In gilded and russet mantle.

The corn has again its mother and she, Leuconoë,
That failed never women,
Fails not the earth now.

The tricksome Hermes is here;
He moves behind me
Eager to catch my words,
Eager to spread them with rumour;
To set upon them his change
Crafty and subtle;
To alter them to his purpose;
But do thou speak true, even to the letter:

" Once more in Delos, once more is the altar
    a-quiver.
Once more is the chant heard.
Once more are the never abandoned gardens
Full of gossip and old tales."

# Preference

It is true that you say the gods are more use to
    you than fairies,
But for all that I have seen you
        on a high, white, noble horse,
Like some strange queen in a story.

It is odd that you should be covered with long
    robes
        and trailing tendrils and flowers ;
It is odd that you should be changing your face
        and resembling some other woman to ,
        plague me ;
It is odd that you should be hiding yourself
In the cloud of beautiful women who do not
    concern me.

And I, who follow every seed-leaf upon the wind ?
You will say that I deserve this.

# Dance Figure

*For the Marriage in Cana of Galilee*

DARK eyed,
O woman of my dreams,
Ivory sandaled,
There is none like thee among the dancers,
None with swift feet.

I have not found thee in the tents,
In the broken darkness.
I have not found thee at the well-head
Among the women with pitchers.

Thine arms are as a young sapling under the
   bark;
Thy face as a river with lights.

White as an almond are thy shoulders;
As new almonds stripped from the husk.

They guard thee not with eunuchs;
Not with bars of copper.

24

# DANCE FIGURE

Gilt turquoise and silver are in the place of thy
    rest.
A brown robe, with threads of gold woven in
    patterns,
           hast thou gathered about thee,
O Nathat-Ikanaie, "Tree-at-the-river."

As a rillet among the sedge are thy hands upon
    me ;
Thy fingers a frosted stream.

Thy maidens are white like pebbles ;
Their music about thee !

There is none like thee among the dancers ;
None with swift feet.

# April

*Nympharum membra disjecta.*

THREE spirits came to me
And drew me apart
To where the olive boughs
Lay stripped upon the ground:
Pale carnage beneath bright mist.


# Gentildonna

SHE passed and left no quiver in the veins, who
  now
Moving among the trees, and clinging
                         in the air she severed,
Fanning the grass she walked on then, endures:

Grey olive leaves beneath a rain-cold sky.

# The Rest

O HELPLESS few in my country,
O remnant enslaved!

Artists broken against her,
A-stray, lost in the villages,
Mistrusted, spoken-against,

Lovers of beauty, starved,
Thwarted with systems,
Helpless against the control;

You who can not wear yourselves out
By persisting to successes,
You who can only speak,
Who can not steel yourselves into reiteration;

You of the finer sense,
Broken against false knowledge,
You who can know at first hand,
Hated, shut in, mistrusted:

Take thought:
I have weathered the storm,
I have beaten out my exile.

# Les Millwin

THE little Millwins attend the Russian Ballet.
The mauve and greenish souls of the little
   Millwins
Were seen lying along the upper seats
Like so many unused boas.

The turbulent and undisciplined host of art
   students—
The rigorous deputation from " Slade "—
Was before them.
With arms exalted, with fore-arms
Crossed in great futuristic X's, the art students
Exulted, they beheld the splendours of *Cleopatra*.

And the little Millwins beheld these things ;
With their large and anæmic eyes they looked
   out upon this configuration.

Let us therefore mention the fact,
For it seems to us worthy of record.

# Further Instructions

COME, my songs, let us express our baser passions,
Let us express our envy of the man with a steady
    job
                    and no worry about the future.
You are very idle, my songs.
I fear you will come to a bad end.
You stand about in the streets,
You loiter at the corners and bus-stops
You do next to nothing at all.

You do not even express our inner nobilities,
You will come to a very bad end.

And I ?
I have gone half cracked,
I have talked to you so much that
                    I almost see you about me,
Insolent  little  beasts,  shameless,  devoid  of
    clothing !

But you, newest song of the lot,
You  are  not  old  enough  to  have  done  much
    mischief,
I will get you a green coat out of China
With dragons worked upon it,
I will get you the scarlet silk trousers
From  the  statue  of  the  infant  Christ  at  Santa
    Maria Novella,
Lest they say we are lacking in taste,
Or that there is no caste in this family.

29

# A Song of the Degrees

## I

REST me with Chinese colours,
For I think the glass is evil.

## II

The wind moves above the wheat—
With a silver crashing,
A thin war of metal.

I have known the golden disc,
I have seen it melting above me.
I have known the stone-bright place,
    The hall of clear colours.

## III

O glass subtly evil, O confusion of colours!
O light bound and bent in, O soul of the captive,
Why am I warned ?   Why am I sent away ?
Why is your glitter full of curious mistrust ?
O glass subtle and cunning, O powdery gold!
O filaments of amber, two-faced iridescence!

# Ite

Go, my songs, seek your praise from the young
  and from the intolerant,
Move among the lovers of perfection alone.
Seek ever to stand in the hard Sophoclean light
And take your wounds from it gladly.

# Dum Capitolium Scandet

How many will come after me
    singing as well as I sing, none better;
Telling the heart of their truth
    as I have taught them to tell it;
Fruit of my seed,
    O my unnameable children.

Know then that I loved you from afore-time,
Clear speakers, naked in the sun, untrammelled.

## To Καλὸν

EVEN in my dreams you have denied yourself to
  me
And sent me only your handmaids.

# The Study in Aesthetics

THE very small children in patched clothing,
Being smitten with an unusual wisdom,
Stopped in their play as she passed them
And cried up from their cobbles:
   *Guarda! Ahi, guarda! ch' è be'a!* \*

But three years after this
I heard the young Dante, whose last name I do
 not know—
For there are, in Sirmione, twenty-eight young
 Dantes and thirty-four Catulli;

And there had been a great catch of sardines,
And his elders
Were packing them in the great wooden boxes
For the market in Brescia, and he
Leapt about, snatching at the bright fish
And getting in both of their ways;
And in vain they commanded him to *sta fermo!*
And when they would not let him arrange
The fish in the boxes
He stroked those which were already arranged,
Murmuring for his own satisfaction
This identical phrase:
   *Ch' è be'a.*

And at this I was mildly abashed.

       *Bella.*

# The Bellaires

*Aus meinen grossen Schmerzen*
*Mach' ich die kleinen Lieder.*

THE good Bellaires
Do not understand the conduct of this world's
affairs.
In fact they understood them so badly
That they have had to cross the Channel.

Nine lawyers, four counsels, five judges and three
proctors of the King,
Together with the respective wives, husbands,
sisters and heterogeneous connections of the
good Bellaires,
Met to discuss their affairs;
But the good Bellaires have so little understood
their affairs
That now there is no one at all
Who can understand any affair of theirs. Yet
Fourteen hunters still eat in the stables of
The good Squire Bellaire;
But these may not suffer attainder,

For they may not belong to the good Squire
    Bellaire
But to his wife.
On the contrary, if they do not belong to his
    wife,
He will plead
A "freedom from attainder"
For twelve horses and also for twelve boarhounds
From Charles the Fourth;
And a further freedom for the remainder
Of horses, from Henry the Fourth.
But the judges,
Being free of mediæval scholarship,
Will pay no attention to this,
And there will be only the more confusion,
Replevin, estoppel, espavin and what not.

Nine lawyers, four counsels, etc.,
Met to discuss their affairs,
But the sole result was bills
From lawyers to whom no one was indebted,
And even the lawyers
Were uncertain who was supposed to be indebted
    to them.

Wherefore the good Squire Bellaire
Resides now at Agde and Biaucaire.
To Carcassonne, Pui, and Alais
He fareth from day to day,

Or takes the sea air
Between Marseilles
And Beziers.

And for all this I have considerable regret,
For the good Bellaires
Are very charming people.


# The New Cake of Soap

Lo, how it gleams and glistens in the sun
Like the cheek of a Chesterton.

# Salvationists

## I

COME, my songs, let us speak of perfection—
We shall get ourselves rather disliked.

## II

Ah yes, my songs, let us resurrect
The very excellent term *Rusticus.*
Let us apply it in all its opprobrium
To those to whom it applies.
And you may decline to make them immortal,
For we shall consider them and their state
In delicate
Opulent silence.

## III

Come, my songs,
Let us take arms against this sea of stupidities—
Begining with Mumpodorus;
And against this sea of vulgarities—
Beginning with Nimmim;
And against this sea of imbeciles—
All the Bulmenian literati.

# Epitaph

LEUCIS, who intended a Grand Passion,
Ends with a willingness-to-oblige.


# Arides

THE bashful Arides
Has married an ugly wife,
He was bored with his manner of life,
Indifferent and discouraged he thought he might
  as
Well do this as anything else.

Saying within his heart, " I am no use to myself,
" Let her, if she wants me, take me."
He went to his doom.

# The Bath Tub

As a bathtub lined with white porcelain,
When the hot water gives out or goes tepid,
So is the slow cooling of our chivalrous passion,
O my much praised but-not-altogether-satis-
factory lady.

# Amitiés

*Old friends the most.*
W. B. Y.

## I

*To one, on returning certain years after.*

You wore the same quite correct clothing,
You took no pleasure at all in my triumphs,
You had the same old air of condescension
Mingled with a curious fear
    That I, myself, might have enjoyed them.

*Te voilà, mon Bourrienne,* you    also    shall    be
    immortal.

## II

*To another.*

And we say good-bye to you also,
For you seem never to have discovered
That your relationship is wholly parasitic ;
Yet to our feasts you bring neither
Wit, nor good spirits, nor the pleasing attitudes
    Of discipleship.

39

# AMITIÉS

## III

But you, *bos amic,* we keep on,
For to you we owe a real debt:
In spite of your obvious flaws,
You once discovered a moderate chop-house.

## IV

*Iste fuit vir incultus,*
*Deo laus, quod est sepultus,*
*Vermes habent eius vultum*
                    *A-a-a-a—A-men.*
*Ego autem jovialis*
*Gaudero contubernalis*
*Cum jocunda femina.*

# Meditatio

WHEN I carefully consider the curious habits of
  dogs
I am compelled to conclude
That man is the superior animal.

When I consider the curious habits of man
I confess, my friend, I am puzzled.

# To  Dives

WHO am I to condemn you, O Dives,
I who am as much embittered
With poverty
As you are with useless riches ?

# Ladies

*Agathas.*

FOUR and forty lovers had Agathas in the old
    days,
All of whom she refused;
And now she turns to me seeking love,
And her hair also is turning.

*Young Lady.*

I have fed your lar with poppies,
I have adored you for three full years;
And now you grumble because your dress does
    not fit
And because I happen to say so.

*Lesbia Illa*

Memnon, Memnon, that lady
Who used to walk about amongst us
With such gracious uncertainty,
Is now wedded
To a British householder.
*Lugete, Veneres! Lugete, Cupidinesque!*

# LADIES

## *Passing*

Flawless as Aphrodite,
Thoroughly beautiful,
Brainless,
The faint odour of your patchouli,
Faint, almost, as the lines of cruelty about your
    chin,
Assails me, and concerns me almost as little.

# Phyllidula

PHYLLIDULA is scrawny but amorous,
Thus have the gods awarded her
That in pleasure she receives more than she can
  give,
If she does not count this blessed
Let her change her religion.

# The Patterns

ERINNA is a model parent,
Her children have never discovered her adulteries.

Lalage is also a model parent,
Her offspring are fat and happy.

# Coda

O MY songs,
Why do you look so eagerly and so curiously into
  people's faces,
Will you find your lost dead among them ?

# The Seeing Eye

THE small dogs look at the big dogs;
They observe unwieldy dimensions
And curious imperfections of odour.

Here is a formal male group:
The young men look upon their seniors,
They consider the elderly mind
And observe its inexplicable correlations.

Said Tsin-Tsu:
It is only in small dogs and the young
That we find minute observation.

45

# Ancora

Good God! They say you are *risqué*,
O canzonetti!
We who went out into the four A.M. of the world
Composing our albas,
We who shook off our dew with the rabbits,
We who have seen even Artemis a-binding her
  sandals,
Have we ever heard the like?
O mountains of Hellas!!

Gather about me, O Muses!
When we sat upon the granite brink in Helicon
Clothed in the tattered sunlight,
O Muses with delicate shins,
O Muses with delectable knee-joints,
When we splashed and were splashed with
The lucid Castalian spray,
Had we ever such an epithet cast upon us!!

46

# A TRANSLATION

FROM THE PROVENÇAL OF EN BERTRANS DE BORN.

## "Dompna pois de me no'us cal"

LADY, since you care nothing for me,
And since you have shut me away from you
Causelessly,
I know not where to go seeking,
For certainly
I will never again gather
Joy so rich, and if I find not ever
A lady with look so speaking
To my desire, worth yours whom I have lost,
I'll have no other love at any cost.

And since I could not find a peer to you,
Neither one so fair, nor of such heart,
So eager and alert,
Nor with such art
In attire, nor so gay
Nor with gift so bountiful and so true,

47

## "DOMPNA POIS DE ME NO'US CAL"

I will go out a-searching,
Culling from each a fair trait
To make me a borrowed lady
Till I again find you ready.

Bels Cembelins, I take of you your colour,
For it's your own, and your glance
Where love is,
A proud thing I do here,
For, as to colour and eyes
I shall have missed nothing at all,
Having yours.
I ask of Midons Aelis (of Montfort)
Her straight speech free-running,
That my phantom lack not in cunning.

At Chalais of the Viscountess, I would
That she give me outright
Her two hands and her throat,
So take I my road
To Rochechouart,
Swift-foot to my Lady Anhes,
Seeing that Tristan's lady Iseutz had never
Such grace of locks, I do ye to wit,
Though she'd the far fame for it.

Of Audiart at Malemort,
Though she with a full heart
Wish me ill,
I'd have her form that's laced
48

# "DOMPNA POIS DE ME NO'US CAL"

So cunningly,
Without blemish, for her love
Breaks not nor turns aside.
I of Miels-de-ben demand
Her straight fresh body,
She is so supple and young,
Her robes can but do her wrong.

Her white teeth, of the Lady Faidita
I ask, and the fine courtesy
She hath to welcome one,
And such replies she lavishes
Within her nest;
Of Bels Mirals, the rest,
Tall stature and gaiety,
To make these avail
She knoweth well, betide
No change nor turning aside.

Ah, Bels Senher, Maent, at last
I ask naught from you,
Save that I have such hunger for
This phantom
As I've for you, such flame-lap,
And yet I'd rather
Ask of you than hold another,
Mayhap, right close and kissed.
Ah, lady, why have you cast
Me out, knowing you hold me so fast!

# The Coming of War: Actaeon

AN image of Lethe,
            and the fields
Full of faint light
            but golden,
Gray cliffs,
            and beneath them
A sea
Harsher than granite,
            unstill, never ceasing;
High forms
            with the movement of gods,
Perilous aspect;
            And one said:
" This is Actaeon."
            Actaeon of golden greaves!

Over fair meadows,
Over the cool face of that field,
Unstill, ever moving,
Hosts of an ancient people,
The silent cortège.

# After Ch'u Yuan

I WILL get me to the wood
Where the gods walk garlanded in wistaria,
By the silver blue flood
   move others with ivory cars.
There come forth many maidens
   to gather grapes for the leopards, my friend,
For there are leopards drawing the cars.

I will walk in the glade,
I will come out of the new thicket
   and accost the procession of maidens.


# Liu Ch'e

THE rustling of the silk is discontinued,
Dust drifts over the court-yard,
There is no sound of foot-fall, and the leaves
Scurry into heaps and lie still,
And she the rejoicer of the heart is beneath
   them:

A wet leaf that clings to the threshold.

# Fan-piece, for her Imperial Lord

O FAN of white silk,
      clear as frost on the grass-blade,
You also are laid aside.

# Ts'ai Chi'h

THE petals fall in the fountain,
      the orange-coloured rose-leaves,
Their ochre clings to the stone.

# In a Station of the Metro

THE apparition of these faces in the crowd ;
Petals on a wet, black bough.

# Alba

As cool as the pale wet leaves
                         of lily-of-the-valley
She lay beside me in the dawn.

# Heather

THE black panther treads at my side,
And above my fingers
There float the petal-like flames.

The milk-white girls
Unbend from the holly-trees,
And their snow-white leopard
Watches to follow our trace.

HA ! sir, I have seen you sniffing and snoozling
  about
                              among my flowers.
And what, pray, do you know about horticulture,
                              you capriped ?

"Come, Auster, come, Apeliota,
And see the faun in our garden.
But if you move or speak
This thing will run at you
And scare itself to spasms."


## Coitus

THE gilded phaloi of the crocuses
            are thrusting at the spring air.
Here is there naught of dead gods
But a procession of festival,
A procession, O Giulio Romano,
Fit for your spirit to dwell in.
Dione, your nights are upon us.

The dew is upon the leaf.
The night about us is restless.

54

# The Encounter

ALL the while they were talking the new morality
Her eyes explored me.
And when I arose to go
Her fingers were like the tissue
Of a Japanese paper napkin.

# Tempora

Io! Io! Tamuz!
The Dryad stands in my court-yard
With plaintive, querulous crying.
(Tamuz. Io! Tamuz!)
Oh, no, she is not crying : " Tamuz."
She says, " May my poems be printed this week ?
The god Pan is afraid to ask you,
May my poems be printed this week ? "

# Black Slippers : Bellotti

AT the table beyond us
With her little suede slippers off,
With her white-stocking'd feet
Carefully kept from the floor by a napkin,
She converses :
                    *Connaissez-vous Ostende?*
The gurgling Italian lady on the other side of the
    restaurant
Replies with a certain hauteur,
But I await with patience
To see how Celestine will re-enter her slippers.
She re-enters them with a groan.


# Society

THE family position was waning,
And on this account the little Aurelia,
Who had laughed on eighteen summers,
Now bears the palsied contact of Phidippus.

## Image from D'Orleans

Young men riding in the street
In the bright new season
Spur without reason,
Causing their steeds to leap.

And at the pace they keep
Their horses' armoured feet
Strike sparks from the cobbled street
In the bright new season.

## Papyrus

Spring. . .
Too long. . .
Gongula. . .

## "Ione, Dead the Long Year"

Empty are the ways,
Empty are the ways of this land
And the flowers
                Bend over with heavy heads.
They bend in vain.
Empty are the ways of this land
                Where Ione
Walked once, and now does not walk

But seems like a person just gone.

*ἱμέρρω*

THY soul
Grown delicate with satieties,
Atthis.

                              O Atthis,
I long for thy lips.

I long for thy narrow breasts,
Thou restless, ungathered.


## Shop Girl

FOR a moment she rested against me
Like a swallow half blown to the wall,
And they talk of Swinburne's women,
And the shepherdess meeting with Guido,
And the harlots of Baudelaire.

# To Formianus' Young Lady Friend

AFTER VALERIUS CATULLUS

ALL Hail! young lady with a nose
         by no means too small,
With a foot unbeautiful,
         and with eyes that are not black,
With fingers that are not long, and with a mouth
   undry,
And with a tongue by no means too elegant,
You are the friend of Formianus, the vendor of
   cosmetics,
And they call you beautiful in the province,
And you are even compared to Lesbia.

O most unfortunate age!

# Tame Cat

" It rests me to be among beautiful women.
Why should one always lie about such matters ?

I repeat :
It rests me to converse with beautiful women
Even though we talk nothing but nonsense,

The purring of the invisible antennæ
Is both stimulating and delightful."


# L'Art, 1910

Green arsenic smeared on an egg-white cloth,
Crushed strawberries! Come, let us feast our
eyes.

# Simulacra

WHY does the horse-faced lady of just the un-
mentionable age
Walk down Longacre reciting Swinburne to herself,
inaudibly ?
Why does the small child in the soiled-white
imitation fur coat
Crawl in the very black gutter beneath the grape
stand ?
Why does the really handsome young woman
approach me in Sackville Street
Undeterred by the manifest age of my trappings ?


# Women Before a Shop

THE gew-gaws of false amber and false turquoise
attract them.
" Like to like nature " : these agglutinous
yellows !

# Epilogue

O CHANSONS foregoing
You were a seven days' wonder,
When you came out in the magazines
You created considerable stir in Chicago,

And now you are stale and worn out,
You're a very depleted fashion,
A hoop-skirt, a calash,
An homely, transient antiquity.

Only emotion remains.

Your emotions ?
                    Are those of a maître-de-café.

# The Social Order

## I

THIS government official,
Whose wife is several years his senior,
Has such a caressing air
When he shakes hands with young ladies.

## II

(Pompes Funèbres)

This old lady,
Who was "so old that she was an atheist,"
Is now surrounded
By six candles and a crucifix,
While the second wife of a nephew
Makes hay with the things in her house.
Her two cats
Go before her into Avernus;
A sort of chloroformed suttee,
And it is to be hoped that their spirits will walk
With their tails up,
And with a plaintive, gentle mewing,
For it is certain that she has left on this earth
No sound
Save a squabble of female connections.

# The Tea Shop

THE girl in the tea shop
                 is not so beautiful as she was,
The August has worn against her.
She does not get up the stairs so eagerly,
Yes, she also will turn middle-aged,
And the glow of youth that she spread about us
                 as she brought us our muffins
Will be spread about us no longer.
                 She also will turn middle-aged.

# Epitaphs

## Fu I

Fu I loved the high cloud and the hill,
Alas, he died of alcohol.

## Li Po

And Li Po also died drunk.
He tried to embrace a moon
In the Yellow River.

# Our Contemporaries

When the Taihaitian princess
Heard that he had decided,
She rushed out into the sunlight and swarmed up
  a cocoanut palm tree,

But he returned to this island
And wrote ninety Petrarchan sonnets.

Note.—Il s'agit d'un jeune poète qui a suivi le culte de
Gauguin jusqu'à Tahiti même (et qui vit encore). Étant
fort bel homme, quand la princesse bistre entendit qu'il voulait
lui accorder ses faveurs elle montra son allegresse de la façon
dont nous venons de parler. Malheureusement ses poèmes ne
sont remplis que de ses propres subjectivités, style Victorien de
la " Georgian Anthology."

# Ancient Wisdom, Rather Cosmic

So-Shu dreamed,
And having dreamed that he was a bird, a bee,
    and a butterfly,
He was uncertain why he should try to feel like
    anything else,

Hence his contentment.

# The Three Poets

Candidia has taken a new lover
And three poets are gone into mourning.
The first has written a long elegy to " Chloris,"
To " Chloris chaste and cold," his " only Chloris."
The second has written a sonnet
                    upon the mutability of woman,
And the third writes an epigram to Candidia.

# The Gipsy

*" Est-ce que vous avez vu des autres—des camarades—avec des singes ou des ours ?"*

A Stray Gipsy—A.D. 1912.

THAT was the top of the walk, when he said:
"Have you seen any others, any of our lot,
" With apes or bears ? "
          —A brown upstanding fellow
Not like the half-castes,
         up on the wet road near Clermont.
The wind came, and the rain,
And mist clotted about the trees in the valley,
And I'd the long ways behind me,
        gray Arles and Biaucaire,
And he said, " Have you seen any of our lot ? "

I'd seen a lot of his lot . . .
        ever since Rhodez,
Coming down from the fair
       of St. John,
With caravans, but never an ape or a bear.

67

# The Game of Chess

DOGMATIC STATEMENT CONCERNING THE GAME OF CHESS:
THEME FOR A SERIES OF PICTURES

RED knights, brown bishops, bright queens,
Striking the board, falling in strong "L"s of
colour,
Reaching and striking in angles,
             holding lines in one colour.
This board is alive with light;
             these pieces are living in form,
Their moves break and reform the pattern:
             Luminous green from the rooks,
Clashing with "X"s of queens,
             looped with the knight-leaps.

"Y" pawns, cleaving, embanking!
Whirl! Centripetal! Mate! King down in the
vortex,
Clash, leaping of bands, straight strips of hard
colour,
Blocked lights working in. Escapes. Renewal of
contest.

# Provincia Deserta

AT Rochecoart,
Where the hills part
    in three ways,
And three valleys, full of winding roads,
Fork out to south and north,
There is a place of trees . . . gray with lichen.
I have walked there
    thinking of old days.
At Chalais
    is a pleached arbour ;
Old pensioners and old protected women
Have the right there—
    it is charity.
I have crept over old rafters,
    peering down
Over the Dronne,
    over a stream full of lilies.
Eastward the road lies,
    Aubeterre is eastward,
With a garrulous old man at the inn.

# PROVINCIA DESERTA

I know the roads in that place :
Mareuil to the north-east,
La Tour,
There are three keeps near Mareuil,
And an old woman,
glad to hear Arnaut,
Glad to lend one dry clothing.

I have walked
into Perigord,
I have seen the torch-flames, high-leaping,
Painting the front of that church,
And, under the dark, whirling laughter.
I have looked back over the stream
and seen the high building,
Seen the long minarets, the white shafts.
I have gone in Ribeyrac
and in Sarlat,
I have climbed rickety stairs, heard talk of Croy,
Walked over En Bertran's old layout,
Have seen Narbonne, and Cahors and Chalus,
Have seen Excideuil, carefully fashioned.

I have said:
" Here such a one walked.
" Here Cœur-de-Lion was slain.
" Here was good singing.
" Here one man hastened his step.
" Here one lay panting."

## PROVINCIA DESERTA

I have looked south from Hautefort,
   thinking of Montaignac, southward.
I have lain in Rocafixada,
   level with sunset,
Have seen the copper come down
   tinging the mountains,
I have seen the fields, pale, clear as an emerald,
Sharp peaks, high spurs, distant castles.
I have said: "The old roads have lain here.
"Men have gone by such and such valleys
"Where the great halls are closer together."
I have seen Foix on its rock, seen Toulouse, and
 Arles greatly altered,
I have seen the ruined "Dorata."
   I have said:
"Riquier! Guido."
   I have thought of the second Troy,
Some little prized place in Auvergnat:
Two men tossing a coin, one keeping a castle,
One set on the highway to sing.
   He sang a woman.
Auvergne rose to the song;
   The Dauphin backed him.
"The castle to Austors!"
   "Pieire kept the singing—
"A fair man and a pleasant."
   He won the lady,
Stole her away for himself, kept her against
 armed force:

## PROVINCIA DESERTA

So ends that story.
That age is gone ;
Pieire de Maensac is gone.
I have walked over these roads ;
I have thought of them living.

# CATHAY

FOR THE MOST PART FROM THE CHINESE OF RIHAKU,
FROM THE NOTES OF THE LATE ERNEST
FENOLLOSA, AND THE DECIPHERINGS
OF THE PROFESSORS MORI
AND ARIGA

# Song of the Bowmen of Shu

HERE we are, picking the first fern-shoots
And saying: When shall we get back to our
country?
Here we are because we have the Ken-nin for our
foemen,
We have no comfort because of these Mongols.
We grub the soft fern-shoots,
When anyone says "Return," the others are full
of sorrow.
Sorrowful minds, sorrow is strong, we are hungry
and thirsty.
Our defence is not yet made sure, no one can let
his friend return.
We grub the old fern-stalks.
We say: Will we be let to go back in October?
There is no ease in royal affairs, we have no
comfort.
Our sorrow is bitter, but we would not return to
our country.
What flower has come into blossom?
Whose chariot? The General's.

75

# SONG OF THE BOWMEN OF SHU

Horses, his horses even, are tired. They were
strong.
We have no rest, three battles a month.
By heaven, his horses are tired.
The generals are on them, the soldiers are by
them
The horses are well trained, the generals have
ivory arrows and quivers ornamented with fish-
skin.
The enemy is swift, we must be careful.
When we set out, the willows were drooping with
spring,
We come back in the snow,
We go slowly, we are hungry and thirsty,
Our mind is full of sorrow, who will know of our
grief ?

*By Bunno.*
· *Very early.*

# The Beautiful Toilet

BLUE, blue is the grass about the river
And the willows have overfilled the close garden.
And within, the mistress, in the midmost of her
  youth,
White, white of face, hesitates, passing the door.
Slender, she puts forth a slender hand,

And she was a courtezan in the old days,
And she has married a sot,
Who now goes drunkenly out
And leaves her too much alone.

*By Mei Sheng.*
*B.C. 140.*

# The River Song

THIS boat is of shato-wood, and its gunwales are
    cut magnolia,
Musicians with jewelled flutes and with pipes of
    gold
Fill full the sides in rows, and our wine
Is rich for a thousand cups.
We carry singing girls, drift with the drifting
    water,
Yet Sennin needs
A yellow stork for a charger, and all our seamen
Would follow the white gulls or ride them.
Kutsu's prose song
Hangs with the sun and moon.

King So's terraced palace
                    is now but a barren hill,
But I draw pen on this barge
Causing the five peaks to tremble,
And I have joy in these words
                    like the joy of blue islands.
(If glory could last forever

Then the waters of Han would flow northward.)
And I have moped in the Emperor's garden,
    awaiting an order-to-write!
I looked at the dragon-pond, with its willow-
    coloured water
Just reflecting the sky's tinge,
And heard the five-score nightingales aimlessly
    singing.

The eastern wind brings the green colour into the
    island grasses at Yei-shu,
The purple house and the crimson are full of
    Spring softness.
South of the pond the willow-tips are half-blue
    and bluer,
Their cords tangle in mist, against the brocade-
    like palace.
Vine-strings a hundred feet long hang down from
    carved railings,
And high over the willows, the fine birds sing to
    each other, and listen,
Crying—"Kwan, Kuan," for the early wind, and
    the feel of it.
The wind bundles itself into a bluish cloud and
    wanders off.
Over a thousand gates, over a thousand doors are
    the sounds of spring singing,
And the Emperor is at Ko.
Five clouds hang aloft, bright on the purple sky,

# THE RIVER SONG

The imperial guards come forth from the golden
house with their armour a-gleaming.
The Emperor in his jewelled car goes out to
inspect his flowers,
He goes out to Hori, to look at the wing-flapping
storks,
He returns by way of Sei rock, to hear the new
nightingales,
For the gardens at Jo-run are full of new nightin-
gales,
Their sound is mixed in this flute,
Their voice is in the twelve pipes here.

*By Rihaku.*
*8th century A.D.*

# The River-Merchant's Wife: a Letter

WHILE my hair was still cut straight across my
    forehead
I played about the front gate, pulling flowers
You came by on bamboo stilts, playing horse,
You walked about my seat, playing with blue
    plums.
And we went on living in the village of Chokan:
Two small people, without dislike or suspicion.

At fourteen I married My Lord you.
I never laughed, being bashful.
Lowering my head, I looked at the wall.
Called to, a thousand times, I never looked back.

At fifteen I stopped scowling,
I desired my dust to be mingled with yours
Forever and forever, and forever.
Why should I climb the look out?

At sixteen you departed,
You went into far Ku-to-Yen, by the river of
    swirling eddies,

# THE RIVER MERCHANT'S WIFE

And you have been gone five months.
The monkeys make sorrowful noise overhead.
You dragged your feet when you went out.
By the gate now, the moss is grown, the different
   mosses,
Too deep to clear them away!
The leaves fall early this autumn, in wind.
The paired butterflies are already yellow with
   August
Over the grass in the West garden,
They hurt me.
I grow older,
If you are coming down through the narrows of
   the river Kiang,
Please let me know beforehand,
And I will come out to meet you,
                    As far as Cho-fu-Sa.

*By Rihaku.*

# The Jewel Stairs' Grievance

THE jewelled steps are already quite white with
dew,
It is so late that the dew soaks my gauze
stockings,
And I let down the crystal curtain
And watch the moon through the clear autumn.

*By Rihaku.*

NOTE.—Jewel stairs, therefore a palace. Grievance, therefore there is something to complain of. Gauze stockings, therefore a court lady, not a servant who complains. Clear autumn,
therefore he has no excuse on account of weather. Also she has
come early, for the dew has not merely whitened the stairs, but
has soaked her stockings. The poem is especially prized because
she utters no direct reproach.

# Poem by the Bridge at Ten-Shin

MARCH has come to the bridge head,
Peach boughs and apricot boughs hang over a
    thousand gates,
At morning there are flowers to cut the heart,
And evening drives them on the eastward-flowing
    waters.
Petals are on the gone waters and on the going,
            And on the back-swirling eddies,
But to-day's men are not the men of the old days,
Though they hang in the same way over the
    bridge-rail.

The sea's colour moves at the dawn
And the princes still stand in rows, about the
    throne,
And the moon falls over the portals of Sei-go-yo,
And clings to the walls and the gate-top.
With head gear glittering against the cloud and
    sun,
The lords go forth from the court, and into far
    borders.

84

# POEM BY THE BRIDGE AT TEN-SHIN

They ride upon dragon-like horses,
Upon horses with head-trappings of yellow metal,
And the streets make way for their passage.
   Haughty their passing,
Haughty their steps as they go into great
 banquets,
To high halls and curious food,
To the perfumed air and girls dancing,
To clear flutes and clear singing ;
To the dance of the seventy couples ;
To the mad chase through the gardens.
Night and day are given over to pleasure
And they think it will last a thousand autumns,
   Unwearying autumns.
For them the yellow dogs howl portents in vain,
And what are they compared to the lady
 Riokushu,
   That was cause of hate !
Who among them is a man like Han-rei
   Who departed alone with his mistress,
With her hair unbound, and he his own skiffs-
 man !

*By Rihaku.*

# Lament of the Frontier Guard

By the North Gate, the wind blows full of sand,
Lonely from the beginning of time until now!
Trees fall, the grass goes yellow with autumn.
I climb the towers and towers
       to watch out the barbarous land:
Desolate castle, the sky, the wide desert.
There is no wall left to this village.
Bones white with a thousand frosts,
High heaps, covered with trees and grass;
Who brought this to pass?
Who has brought the flaming imperial anger?
Who has brought the army with drums and with
    kettle-drums?
Barbarous kings.
A gracious spring, turned to blood-ravenous
    autumn,
A turmoil of wars-men, spread over the middle
    kingdom,
Three hundred and sixty thousand,
And sorrow, sorrow like rain.
Sorrow to go, and sorrow, sorrow returning,

# LAMENT OF THE FRONTIER GUARD

Desolate, desolate fields,
And no children of warfare upon them,
    No longer the men for offence and defence.
Ah, how shall you know the dreary sorrow at the
    North Gate,
With Rihoku's name forgotten,
And we guardsmen fed to the tigers.

*By Rihaku.*

# Exile's Letter

To So-Kin of Rakuyo, ancient friend, Chancellor
    of Gen.
Now I remember that you built me a special tavern
By the south side of the bridge at Ten-Shin.
With yellow gold and white jewels, we paid for
    songs and laughter
And we were drunk for month on month, forgetting
    the kings and princes.
Intelligent men came drifting in from the sea and
    from the west border,
And with them, and with you especially
There was nothing at cross purpose,
And they made nothing of sea-crossing or of
    mountain crossing,
If only they could be of that fellowship,
And we all spoke out our hearts and minds, and
    without regret.

And then I was sent off to South Wei,
        smothered in laurel groves,
And you to the north of Raku-hoku,
Till we had nothing but thoughts and memories
    in common.

And then, when separation had come to its
    worst,
We met, and travelled into Sen-Go,
Through all the thirty-six folds of the turning
    and twisting waters,
Into a valley of the thousand bright flowers,
That was the first valley;
And into ten thousand valleys full of voices and
    pine-winds.
And with silver harness and reins of gold,
Out come the East of Kan foreman and his
    company.
And there came also the " True man " of Shi-yo
    to meet me,
Playing on a jewelled mouth-organ.
In the storied houses of San-Ko they gave us
    more Sennin music,
Many instruments, like the sound of young
    phoenix broods.
The foreman of Kan Chu, drunk, danced
            because his long sleeves wouldn't
            keep still
With that music playing.
And I, wrapped in brocade, went to sleep with
    my head on his lap,
And my spirit so high it was all over the
    heavens,
And before the end of the day we were scattered
    like stars, or rain.

I had to be off to So, far away over the waters,
You back to your river-bridge.

And your father, who was brave as a leopard,
Was governor in Hei Shu, and put down the
barbarian rabble.
And one May he had you send for me,
      despite the long distance.
And what with broken wheels and so on, I won't
say it wasn't hard going,
Over roads twisted like sheep's guts.
And I was still going, late in the year,
      in the cutting wind from the North,
And thinking how little you cared for the
cost,
      and you caring enough to pay it.
And what a reception :
Red jade cups, food well set on a blue jewelled
table,
And I was drunk, and had no thought of
returning.
And you would walk out with me to the western
corner of the castle,
To the dynastic temple, with water about it clear
as blue jade,
With boats floating, and the sound of mouth-
organs and drums,
With ripples like dragon-scales, going grass green
on the water,

90

Pleasure lasting, with courtezans, going and com-
ing without hindrance,
With the willow flakes falling like snow,
And the vermilioned girls getting drunk about
sunset,
And the water a hundred feet deep reflecting
green eyebrows
—Eyebrows painted green are a fine sight in
young moonlight,
Gracefully painted—
And the girls singing back at each other,
Dancing in transparent brocade,
And the wind lifting the song, and inter-
rupting it,
Tossing it up under the clouds.
   And all this comes to an end.
   And is not again to be met with.
I went up to the court for examination,
Tried Layu's luck, offered the Choyo song,
And got no promotion,
   and went back to the East Mountains
   white-headed.
And once again, later, we met at the South
bridge-head.
And then the crowd broke up, you went north to
San palace,
And if you ask how I regret that parting:
   It is like the flowers falling at Spring's end
   Confused, whirled in a tangle.

# EXILE'S LETTER

What is the use of talking, and there is no end of
   talking,
There is no end of things in the heart.
I call in the boy,
Have him sit on his knees here
      To seal this,
And send it a thousand miles, thinking.

*By Rihaku.*

*From Rihaku*

## FOUR POEMS OF DEPARTURE

*Light rain is on the light dust*
*The willows of the inn-yard*
*Will be going greener and greener,*
*But you, Sir, had better take wine ere your departure,*
*For you will have no friends about you*
*When you come to the gates of Go.*

# Separation on the River Kiang

KO-JIN goes west from Ko-kaku-ro,
The smoke-flowers are blurred over the river.
His lone sail blots the far sky.
And now I see only the river,
The long Kiang, reaching heaven.

# Taking Leave of a Friend

BLUE mountains to the north of the walls,
White river winding about them ;
Here we must make separation

H

And go out through a thousand miles of dead
grass.
Mind like a floating wide cloud.
Sunset like the parting of old acquaintances
Who bow over their clasped hands at a distance.
Our horses neigh to each other
          as we are departing.


## Leave-taking near Shoku

*" Sanso, King of Shoku, built roads."*

THEY say the roads of Sanso are steep,
Sheer as the mountains.
The walls rise in a man's face,
Clouds grow out of the hill
          at his horse's bridle.
Sweet trees are on the paved way of the Shin,
Their trunks burst through the paving,
And freshets are bursting their ice
          in the midst of Shoku, a proud city.

Men's fates are already set,
There is no need of asking diviners.

# The City of Choan

THE phœnix are at play on their terrace.
The phœnix are gone, the river flows on alone.
Flowers and grass
Cover over the dark path
        where lay the dynastic house of the Go.
The bright cloths and bright caps of Shin
Are now the base of old hills.

The Three Mountains fall through the far heaven,
The isle of White Heron
        splits the two streams apart.
Now the high clouds cover the sun
And I can not see Choan afar
And I am sad.

# South-Folk in Cold Country

THE Dai horse neighs against the bleak wind of
Etsu,
The birds of Etsu have no love for En, in the
north,
Emotion is born out of habit.
Yesterday we went out of the Wild-Goose gate,
To-day from the Dragon-Pen.*
Surprised. Desert turmoil. Sea sun.
Flying snow bewilders the barbarian heaven.
Lice swarm like ants over our accoutrements.
Mind and spirit drive on the feathery banners.
Hard fight gets no reward.
Loyalty is hard to explain.
Who will be sorry for General Rishogu,
        the swift moving,
Whose white head is lost for this province ?

* *I.e.*, we have been warring from one end of the empire to
the other, now east, now west, on each border.

# Sennin Poem by Kakuhaku

THE red and green kingfishers
　　　flash between the orchids and clover,
One bird casts its gleam on another.

Green vines hang through the high forest,
They weave a whole roof to the mountain,
The lone man sits with shut speech,
He purrs and pats the clear strings.

He throws his heart up through the sky,
He bites through the flower pistil
　　　and brings up a fine fountain.
The red-pine-tree god looks on him and wonders.
He rides through the purple smoke to visit the
　　sennin,
He takes " Floating Hill " * by the sleeve,
He claps his hand on the back of the great water
　　sennin.

But you, you dam'd crowd of gnats,
Can you even tell the age of a turtle ?

　　　　　* Name of a sennin.

# A Ballad of the Mulberry Road

(*Fenollosa MSS., very early.*)

THE sun rises in south east corner of things
To look on the tall house of the Shin
For they have a daughter named Rafu,
    (pretty girl)
She made the name for herself: " Gauze Veil,"
For she feeds mulberries to silkworms,
    She gets them by the south wall of the
    town.

With green strings she makes the warp of her
    basket,
She makes the shoulder-straps of her basket
        from the boughs of Katsura,
And she piles her hair up on the left side of her
    head-piece.

Her earrings are made of pearl,
Her underskirt is of green pattern-silk,
Her overskirt is the same silk dyed in purple,
And when men going by look on Rafu
    They set down their burdens,
They stand and twirl their moustaches.

# Old Idea of Choan by Rosoriu

## I.

THE narrow streets cut into the wide highway at
  Choan,
Dark oxen, white horses,
      drag on the seven coaches with outriders.
The coaches are perfumed wood,
The jewelled chair is held up at the crossway,
Before the royal lodge
      a glitter of golden saddles, awaiting the
        princess,
They eddy before the gate of the barons.
The canopy embroidered with dragons
      drinks in and casts back the sun.

Evening comes.
      The trappings are bordered with mist.
The hundred cords of mist are spread through
      and double the trees,
Night birds, and night women,
      spread out their sounds through the
        gardens.

99

# OLD IDEA OF CHOAN BY ROSORIU

## II.

Birds with flowery wing, hovering butterflies
      crowd over the thousand gates,
Trees that glitter like jade,
      terraces tinged with silver,
The seed of a myriad hues,
A net-work of arbours and passages and covered
    ways,
Double towers, winged roofs,
      border the net-work of ways:
A place of felicitous meeting.
Riu's house stands out on the sky,
      with glitter of colour
As Butei of Kan had made the high golden lotus
      to gather his dews,
Before it another house which I do not know:
How shall we know all the friends
      whom we meet on strange roadways?

# To-Em-Mei's "The Unmoving Cloud"

"Wet springtime," says To-em-mei,
"Wet spring in the garden."

## I.

THE clouds have gathered, and gathered,
　　　and the rain falls and falls,
The eight ply of the heavens
　　　are all folded into one darkness,
And the wide, flat road stretches out.
I stop in my room toward the East, quiet, quiet,
I pat my new cask of wine.
My friends are estranged, or far distant,
I bow my head and stand still.

## II

Rain, rain, and the clouds have gathered,
The eight ply of the heavens are darkness,
The flat land is turned into river.
　　　"Wine, wine, here is wine!"
I drink by my eastern window.
I think of talking and man,
And no boat, no carriage, approaches.

# TO-EM-MEI'S "THE ÛNMOVING CLOUD"

## III

The trees in my east-looking garden
            are bursting out with new twigs,
They try to stir new affection,

And men say the sun and moon keep on moving
            because they can't find a soft seat.

The birds flutter to rest in my tree,
            and I think I have heard them saying,
" It is not that there are no other men
But we like this fellow the best,
But however we long to speak
He can not know of our sorrow."

*T'ao Yuan Ming.*
*A.D.* 365–427.

END OF CATHAY

# Near Perigord

*A Perigord, pres del muralh*
*Tan que i puosch 'om gitar ab malh.*

You'd have men's hearts up from the dust
And tell their secrets, Messire Cino,
Right enough ?   Then read between the lines
        of Uc St. Cire,
Solve me the riddle, for you know the tale.

Bertrans, En Bertrans, left a fine canzone:
" Maent, I love you, you have turned me out.
The voice at Montfort, Lady Agnes' hair,
Bel Miral's stature, the vicountess' throat,
Set all together, are not worthy of you. . ."
And all the while you sing out that canzone,
Think you that Maent lived at Montaignac,
One at Chalais, another at Malemort
Hard over Brive—for every lady a castle,
Each place strong.

            Oh, *is* it easy enough ?
Tairiran held hall in Montaignac,

His brother-in-law was all there was of power
In Perigord, and this good union
Gobbled all the land, and held it later
      for some hundreds years.
And our En Bertrans was in Altafort,
Hub of the wheel, the stirrer-up of strife,
As caught by Dante in the last wallow of hell—
The headless trunk "that made its head a lamp."
For separation wrought out separation,
And he who set the strife between brother and
    brother
And had his way with the old English king,
Viced in such torture for the "counterpass."

    How would you live, with neighbours set about
      you—
Poictiers and Brive, untaken Rochechouart,
Spread like the finger-tips of one frail hand;
And you on that great mountain of a palm—
Not a neat ledge, not Foix between its streams,
But one huge back half-covered up with pine,
Worked for and snatched from the string-purse of
    Born—
The four round towers, four brothers—mostly
    fools:
What could he do but play the desperate chess,
And stir old grudges ?
            " Pawn your castles, lords !
Let the Jews pay."

# NEAR PERIGORD

And the great scene—
(That, maybe, never happened !)
Beaten at last,
Before the hard old king:
" Your son, ah, since he died
My wit and worth are cobwebs brushed aside
In the full flare of grief.   Do what you will."

Take the whole man, and ravel out the story.
He loved this lady in castle Montaignac ?
The castle flanked him—he had need of it.
You read to-day, how long the overlords of
Perigord,
The Talleyrands, have held the place, it was no
transient fiction.
And Maent failed him ?   Or saw through the
scheme ?

And all his net-like thought of new alliance ?
Chalais is high, a-level with the poplars.
Its lowest stones just meet the valley tips
Where the low Dronne is filled with water-lilies.
And Rochecouart can match it, stronger yet,
The very spur's end, built on sheerest cliff,
And Malemort keeps its close hold on Brive,
While Born his own close purse, his rabbit warren,
His subterranean chamber with a dozen doors,
A-bristle with antennae to feel roads,
To sniff the traffic into Perigord.

And that hard phalanx, that unbroken line,
The ten good miles from thence to Maent's castle,
All of his flank—how could he do without her ?
And all the road to Cahors, to Toulouse ?
What would he do without her ?

           " Papiol,
Go forthright singing—Anhes, Cembelins.
There is a throat ; ah, there are two white hands ;
There is a trellis full of early roses,
And all my heart is bound about with love.
Where am I come with compound flatteries—
What doors are open to fine compliment ? "
And every one half jealous of Maent ?
He wrote the catch to pit their jealousies
Against her, give her pride in them ?

Take his own speech, make what you will of it—
And still the knot, the first knot, of Maent ?

   Is it a love poem ?   Did he sing of war ?
Is it an intrigue to run subtly out,
Born of a jongleur's tongue, freely to pass
Up and about and in and out the land,
Mark him a craftsman and a strategist ?
(St. Leider had done as much at Polhonac,
Singing a different stave, as closely hidden.)
Oh, there is precedent, legal tradition,
To sing one thing when your song means another,

*" Et albirar ab lor bordon—"*
Foix' count knew that.  What is Sir Bertrans'
  singing ?

Maent, Maent, and yet again Maent,
Or war and broken heaumes and politics ?

## II

End fact.  Try fiction,  Let us say we see
En Bertrans, a tower-room at Hautefort,
Sunset, the ribbon-like road lies, in red cross-light,
South   toward  Montaignac,  and  he  bends  at  a
  table
Scribbling, swearing between his teeth, by his left
  hand
Lie little strips of parchment covered over,
Scratched and erased with *al* and *ochaisos*.
Testing his list of rhymes, a lean man ?   Bilious ?
With a red straggling beard ?
And the green cat's-eye lifts toward Montaignac.

Or take his "magnet" singer setting out,
Dodging  his  way  past  Aubeterre,  singing  at
  Chalais
          In the vaulted hall,
Or, by a lichened tree at Rochecouart
Aimlessly watching a hawk above the valleys,
Waiting his turn in the mid-summer evening,

Thinking of Aelis, whom he loved heart and
  soul . . .
To find her half alone, Montfort away,
And a brown, placid, hated woman visiting her,
Spoiling his visit, with a year before the next one.
Little enough ?
Or carry him forward. "Go through all the
  courts,
My Magnet," Bertrand had said.

       We came to Ventadour
In the mid love court, he sings out the canzon,
No one hears save Arrimon Luc D'Esparo—
No one hears aught save the gracious sound of
  compliments.
Sir Arrimon counts on his fingers, Montfort,
Rochecouart, Chalais, the rest, the tactic,
Malemort, guesses beneath, sends word to Cœur
  de Lion :

The compact, de Born smoked out, trees felled
About his castle, cattle driven out !
Or no one sees it, and En Bertrans prospered ?

  And ten years after, or twenty, as you will,
Arnaut and Richard lodge beneath Chalus :
The dull round towers encroaching on the field,
The tents tight drawn, horses at tether
Further and out of reach, the purple night,

# NEAR PERIGORD

The crackling of small fires, the bannerets,
The lazy leopards on the largest banner,
Stray gleams on hanging mail, an armourer's torch-
flare
Melting on steel.

        And in the quietest space
They probe old scandals, say de Born is dead;
And we've the gossip (skipped six hundred years).
Richard shall die to-morrow—leave him there
Talking of *trobar clus* with Daniel.
And the "best craftsman" sings out his friend's
song,
Envies its vigour . . . and deplores the technique,
Dispraises his own skill?—That's as you will.
And they discuss the dead man,
Plantagenet puts the riddle: "Did he love her?"
And Arnaut parries: "Did he love your sister?
True, he has praised her, but in some opinion
He wrote that praise only to show he had
The favour of your party, had been well received."

   "You knew the man."
      "*You* knew the man."
"I am an artist, you have tried both métiers."
"You were born near him."
       "Do we know our friends?"
"Say that he saw the castles, say that he loved
Maent!"

"Say that he loved her, does it solve the riddle?"
End the discussion, Richard goes out next day
And gets a quarrel-bolt shot through his vizard,
Pardons the bowman, dies,

                    Ends our discussion.   Arnaut ends
" In sacred odour "—(that's apocryphal!)
And we can leave the talk till Dante writes :
*Surely I saw, and still before my eyes*
*Goes on that headless trunk, that bears for light*
*Its own head swinging, gripped by the dead hair,*
*And like a swinging lamp that says, " Ah me!*
*I severed men, my head and heart*
*Ye see here severed, my life's counterpart."*

Or take En Bertrans?

### III

*Ed eran due in uno, ed uno in due.*
Inferno, XXVIII, 125.

" Bewildering spring, and by the Auvezere
Poppies and day's-eyes in the green émail
Rose over us ; and we knew all that stream,
And our two horses had traced out the valleys ;
Knew the low flooded lands squared out with
    poplars,
In the young days when the deep sky befriended.

110

And great wings beat above us in the twilight,
And the great wheels in heaven
Bore us together . . . surging . . . and apart . . .
Believing we should meet with lips and hands.

High, high and sure . . . and then the counter-
thrust :
' Why do you love me ?  Will you always love
me ?
But I am like the grass, I can not love you.'
Or, ' Love, and I love and love you,
And hate your mind, not *you,* your soul, your
hands.'

So to this last estrangement, Tairiran !

There shut up in his castle, Tairiran's,
She who had nor ears nor tongue save in her
hands,
Gone—ah, gone—untouched, unreachable !
She who could never live save through one person,
She who could never speak save to one person,
And all the rest of her a shifting change,
A broken bundle of mirrors . . . ! "

# Villanelle: the Psychological Hour

I HAD over-prepared the event,
        that much was ominous.
With middle-ageing care
        I had laid out just the right books.
I had almost turned down the pages.

                *Beauty is so rare a thing.*
                *So few drink of my fountain.*


So much barren regret,
So many hours wasted!
And now I watch, from the window,
        the rain, the wandering busses.

" Their little cosmos is shaken "—
        the air is alive with that fact.
In their parts of the city
        they are played on by diverse forces.
How do I know?
        Oh, I know well enough.
For them there is something afoot.

112

# VILLANELLE

As for me:
I had over-prepared the event—

*Beauty is so rare a thing.*
*So few drink of my fountain.*

Two friends: a breath of the forest . . .
Friends ?  Are people less friends
        because  one  has  just,  at  least,  found
        them ?
Twice they promised to come.
    *" Between the night and morning ? "*

*Beauty would drink of my mind.*
Youth would awhile forget
        my youth is gone from me.


## II

(" Speak up !  You have danced so stiffly ?
    Someone admired your works,
    And said so frankly.

    " Did you talk like a fool,
    The first night ?
    The second evening ? "

" *But* they promised again:
        ' To-morrow at tea-time.' ")
113

# VILLANELLE

## III

Now the third day is here—
    no word from either;
No word from her nor him,
Only another man's note:
    "Dear Pound, I am leaving England."

# Dans un Omnibus de Londres

Les yeux d'une morte aimée
M'ont salué,
Enchassés dans un visage stupide
Dont tous les autres traits étaient banals,
Ils m'ont salué

Et alors je vis bien des choses
Au dedans de ma mémoire
Remuer,
S'éveiller.

Je vis des canards sur le bord d'un lac minuscule,
Auprès d'un petit enfant gai, bossu.

Je vis les colonnes anciennes en " toc "
Du Parc Monceau,
Et deux petites filles graciles,
Des patriciennes,
         aux toisons couleur de lin,
Et des pigeonnes
Grasses
      comme des poulardes.

115

# DANS UN OMNIBUS DE LONDRES

Je vis le parc,
Et tous les gazons divers
Où nous avions loué des chaises
Pour quatre sous.

Je vis les cygnes noirs,
Japonais,
Leurs ailes
Teintées de couleur sang-de-dragon,

Et toutes les fleurs
D'Armenonville.

Les yeux d'une morte
M'ont salué.

# To a Friend Writing on Cabaret Dancers

*" Breathe not the word to-morrow in her ears."*
Vir Quidem, on Dancers.

GOOD "Hedgethorn," for we'll anglicize your
name
Until the last slut's hanged and the last pig
disemboweled,
Seeing your wife is charming and your child
Sings in the open meadow—at least the kodak
says so—
My good fellow, you, on a cabaret silence
And the dancers, you write a sonnet,
Say "Forget To-morrow," being of all men
The most prudent, orderly, and decorous !

"Pepita" has no to-morrow, so you write.

Pepita has such to-morrows: with the hands
puffed out,
The pug-dog's features encrusted with tallow
Sunk in a frowsy collar—an unbrushed black.
She will not bathe too often, but her jewels

117

## CABARET DANCERS

Will be a stuffy, opulent sort of fungus
Spread on both hands and on the up-pushed
bosom—
It juts like a shelf between the jowl and corset.

Have you, or I seen most of cabarets, good
Hedgethorn ?

Here's Pepita, tall and slim as an Egyptian
mummy,
Marsh-cranberries, the ribbed and angular pods
Flare up with scarlet orange on stiff stalks
And so Pepita
        flares on the crowded stage before our
        tables
Or slithers about between the dishonest waiters—
        " Carmen est maigre, un trait de bistre
        Cerne son œil de gitana "

And " rend la flamme "
        you know the deathless verses.
I search the features, the avaricious features
Pulled by the kohl and rouge out of resemblance—
Six pence the object for a change of passion.

" Write me a poem."
        Come now, my dear Pepita,
"-ita, bonita, chiquita,"
        that's what you mean you advertising
        spade,

118

Or take the intaglio, my fat great-uncle's heir-
    loom :
Cupid, astride a phallus with two wings,
Swinging a cat-o'-nine-tails.
                No.   Pepita,
I have seen through the crust.
            I don't know what you look like
But your smile pulls one way
            and your painted grin another,
While that cropped fool,
            that tom-boy who can't earn her living.
Come, come to-morrow,
            To-morrow in ten years at the latest,
She will be drunk in the ditch, but you, Pepita,
Will be quite rich, quite plump, with pug-bitch
    features,
With a black tint staining your cuticle,
Prudent and svelte Pepita.
            " Poète, writ me a poème ! "
Spanish and Paris, love of the arts part of your
            geisha-culture !

Euhenia, in short skirts, slaps her wide stomach,
Pulls up a roll of fat for the pianist,
" Pauvre femme maigre ! " she says.
            He sucks his chop bone,
That some one else has paid for,
            grins up an amiable grin,
Explains the decorations.

# CABARET DANCERS

Good Hedgethorn, they all have futures,
All these people.
Old Popkoff
Will dine next week with Mrs. Basil,
Will meet a duchess and an ex-diplomat's widow
From Weehawken—who has never known
Any but " Majesties " and Italian nobles.

Euhenia will have a *fonda* in Orbajosa.
The amorous nerves will give way to digestive ;
" Delight thy soul in fatness," saith the preacher.
We can't preserve the elusive "*mica salis*,"
It may last well in these dark northern climates,
Nell Gwynn's still here, despite the reformation,
And Edward's mistresses still light the stage,
A glamour of classic youth in their deportment.
The prudent whore is not without her future,
Her bourgeois dulness is deferred.
Her present dulness . . .

Oh well, her present dulness . . .

Now in Venice, 'Storante al Giardino, I went early,
Saw the performers come : him, her, the baby,
A quiet and respectable-tawdry trio ;
An hour later : a show of calves and spangles,

" *Un e due fanno tre*,"
Night after night,
No change, no change of program, " *Chè !*
La donna è mobile.*"

# Homage to Quintus Septimius Florentis Christianus

(*Ex libris Graecae*)

## I

THEODORUS will be pleased at my death,
And someone else will be pleased at the death of
    Theodorus,
And yet everyone speaks evil of death.

## II

This place is the Cyprian's, for she has ever the
    fancy
To be looking out across the bright sea,
Therefore the sailors are cheered, and the waves
Keep small with reverence, beholding her image.

Anyte.

## III

A sad and great evil is the expectation of death—
And there are also the inane expenses of the
    funeral;
Let us therefore cease from pitying the dead
For after death there comes no other calamity.

Palladas.

121

HOMAGE

## IV

*Troy*

Whither, O city, are your profits and your gilded
  shrines,
And your barbecues of great oxen,
And the tall women walking your streets, in gilt
  clothes,
With their perfumes in little alabaster boxes ?
Where is the work of your home-born sculptors ?

Time's tooth is into the lot, and war's and fate's
  too.
Envy has taken your all,
Save your douth and your story.

                              *Agathas Scholasticus.*

## V

Woman ?   Oh, woman is a consummate rage,
         but dead, or asleep, she pleases.
Take her.   She has two excellent seasons.

                                        *Palladas.*

## VI

*Nicharcus upon Phidon his doctor*

Phidon neither purged me, nor touched me,
But I remembered the name of his fever medicine
                              and died.

# Fish and the Shadow

THE salmon-trout drifts in the stream,
The soul of the salmon-trout floats over the
stream
         Like a little wafer of light.

The salmon moves in the sun-shot, bright shallow
sea. . . .

As light as the shadow of the fish
         that falls through the water,
She came into the large room by the stair,
Yawning a little she came with the sleep still
upon her.

"I am just from bed. The sleep is still in my
eyes.
"Come. I have had a long dream."

And I: "That wood?
And two springs have passed us."

123

# FISH AND THE SHADOW

" Not so far, no, not so far now,
There is a place—but no one else knows it—
A field in a valley . . .

*Qu'ieu sui avinen,*

*Ieu lo sai.*"

She must speak of the time
Of Arnaut de Mareuil, I thought, " *qu'ieu sui
avinen.*"

Light as the shadow of the fish
That falls through the pale green water.